The Alamo and the Birth of Texas

Copyright © 2025 by JSB Morse. All Rights Reserved. Printed in the United States of America.

This book was produced by Libertas Kids, an imprint of Code Publishing, Boerne, Texas. LibertasKids.com
Paperback ISBN 9781600201462 Hardcover ISBN 9781600201486 Ebook ISBN 9781600201479

In 1709, Franciscan Antonio de San Buenaventura y Olivares joined an expedition into the New Spain region of Texas, meaning 'friend' in the Native tongue. Recognizing its potential for settlement, he later traveled to Spain to convince authorities of the importance of establishing missions in the area. After years of persistence, Fray Olivares gained approval, and he returned to Texas to found Misión San Antonio de Valero, named for St. Anthony of Padua and the Viceroy of New Spain, the Marquess of Valero.

This mission became a place where Franciscan missionaries and Native American converts lived and worked together, learning about faith, farming, and community. For over 70 years, the mission thrived as a center of faith and community.

In 1793, everything changed. The Spanish government decided to secularize the missions, meaning they were no longer run by the church. The lands and buildings of San Antonio de Valero were given to local residents. The mission's chapel stood empty for a time, but its story was far from over.

In the early 1800s, Spanish soldiers began using the chapel as a fort. They called it El Alamo, which means "cottonwood" in Spanish, because of the cottonwood trees nearby. It was also named after their hometown, Alamo de Parras, in Mexico.

In 1821, Agustín de Iturbide led a successful revolt against Spanish rule, rallying supporters with the cry, "¡Viva la independencia! ¡Viva la libertad!" Iturbide's efforts brought an end to Spain's control, and Mexico became an independent nation. This was a time of great hope and change, as the people of Mexico sought to build a country founded on freedom and independence. Yet the vast northern regions of Mexico, including Texas, remained sparsely populated and vulnerable to outside threats.

To strengthen its northern territories, the new Mexican government invited settlers from the United States to move to the Texas region. Many accepted this offer, drawn by the promise of land and opportunity.

Among them was Stephen F. Austin, who brought hundreds of families to Texas. These settlers built communities, farms, and towns, helping to transform the region into a thriving frontier. But this influx of settlers would also sow the seeds of future conflicts between the Mexican government and the growing population of Anglo-Americans in Texas.

As more settlers arrived, tensions grew. By 1830, the Mexican government, worried about losing control, passed laws to limit American immigration to Texas. Conflicts broke out, like the Anahuac Disturbance and the Battle of Velasco in 1832, where settlers and Mexican officials clashed.

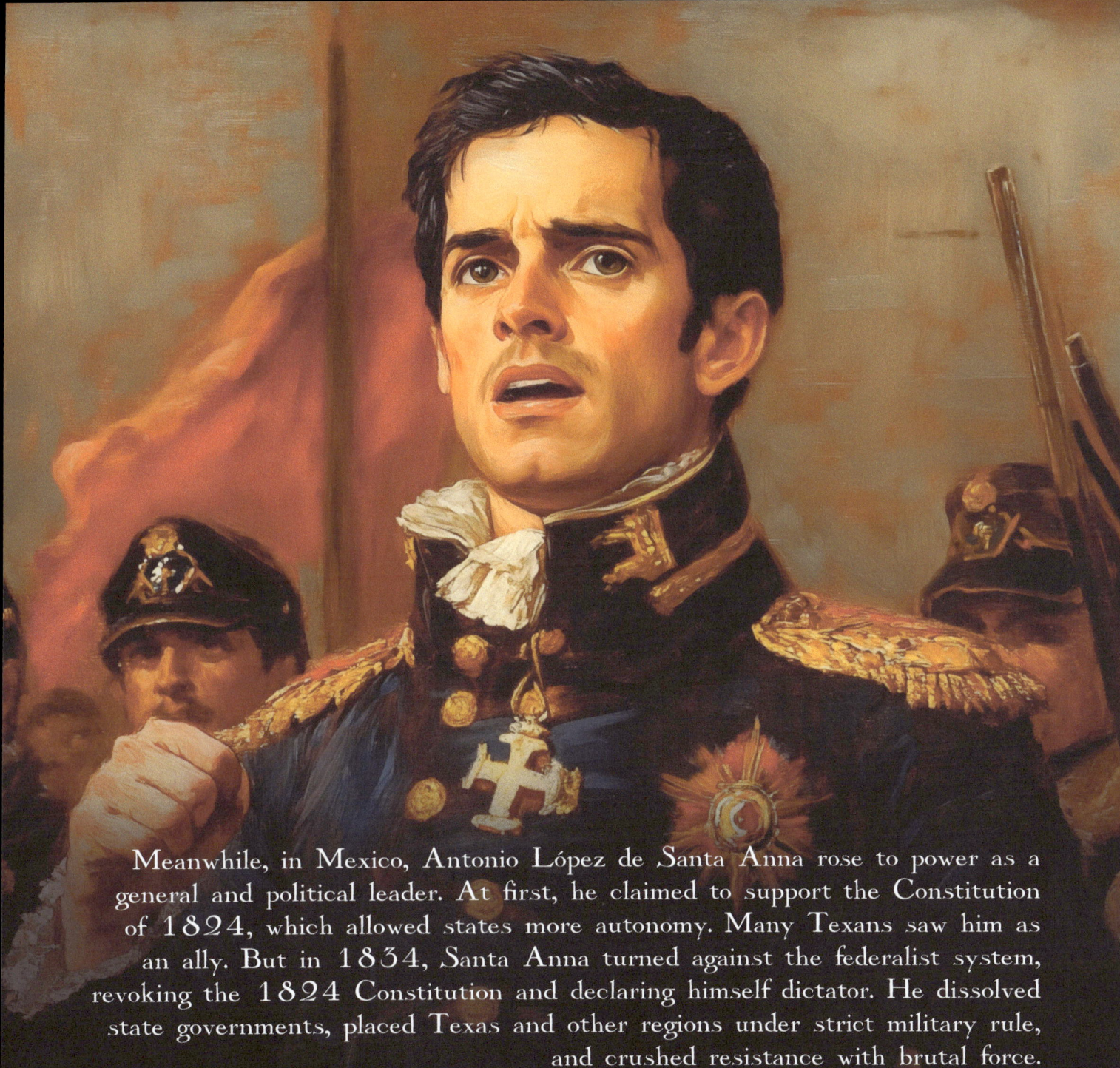

Meanwhile, in Mexico, Antonio López de Santa Anna rose to power as a general and political leader. At first, he claimed to support the Constitution of 1824, which allowed states more autonomy. Many Texans saw him as an ally. But in 1834, Santa Anna turned against the federalist system, revoking the 1824 Constitution and declaring himself dictator. He dissolved state governments, placed Texas and other regions under strict military rule, and crushed resistance with brutal force.

In 1835, Texans decided they could no longer live under Santa Anna's rule. The first skirmish of the Texas Revolution happened in the town of Gonzales, where Mexican soldiers tried to take a cannon from the settlers. The Texans refused, raising a flag that boldly declared, "Come and Take It." They won the skirmish, inspiring more people to join the fight for freedom.

By the end of that year, the Texians had taken control of San Antonio, including the old mission, El Alamo. They turned it into a fortress, preparing to defend their newfound freedom. Legendary frontiersman Davy Crockett and knife fighter James Bowie joined William B. Travis to defend the outpost. They were soon joined by Juan Seguín, who brought a company of Tejano soldiers to fight for Texas independence. Together, these leaders inspired the defenders to stand firm.

In February 1836, Santa Anna's army of over 7,000 troops marched toward San Antonio. On February 23, they surrounded the Alamo. Seeing that the fewer than 200 Texians were vastly outnumbered, Travis sent out Juan Seguín with a letter to the provisional Texas government asking for help. In it, he wrote, "Victory or death." Though Seguín wanted to stay and fight, he obeyed and bravely rode through enemy lines to spread the message, rallying support for the defenders. For 13 days, the Texians held out, despite constant bombardment. Inside the walls, they prayed, planned, and prepared to fight for their freedom.

On March 6, 1836, before dawn, Santa Anna's forces launched a final attack. Most of the noncombatants gathered in the church for safety. Crockett paused briefly in the chapel to say a prayer before running to his post.

The defenders of the Alamo fought bravely, but they were overwhelmingly outnumbered. By sunrise, the battle was over, and all the Texians had fallen as Santa Anna's men took the Alamo.

The devastating loss fueled the Texians' determination. With cries of "Remember the Alamo!" Juan Seguín and others rallied under the leadership of General Sam Houston. Houston, who had once been an honorary member of the Cherokee tribe, had served under Andrew Jackson in the U.S. Army and later as governor of Tennessee. His leadership and experience proved crucial in the fight for Texas independence.

On April 21, 1836, at the Battle of San Jacinto, Houston's small army of 783 surprised Santa Anna's vastly superior forces. The battle lasted only 18 minutes and was a decisive victory for the Texians. Dressed as a common soldier, Santa Anna attempted to flee, but the dictator was taken prisoner the following day.

On May 14, 1836, Santa Anna signed the Treaties of Velasco, recognizing Texas as an independent nation. The Republic of Texas was born, built on the values of faith, freedom, and courage. The Alamo became a symbol of the sacrifices made for liberty.

Today, the Alamo stands as a reminder of the brave souls who fought for freedom. Its walls tell a story of faith, perseverance, and the unyielding desire for independence.

The End

For more great books visit
LibertasKids.com

www.ingramcontent.com/pod-product-compliance
Lightning Source LLC
Chambersburg PA
CBHW041603070526
44586CB00003BA/64